T Is for Toscana

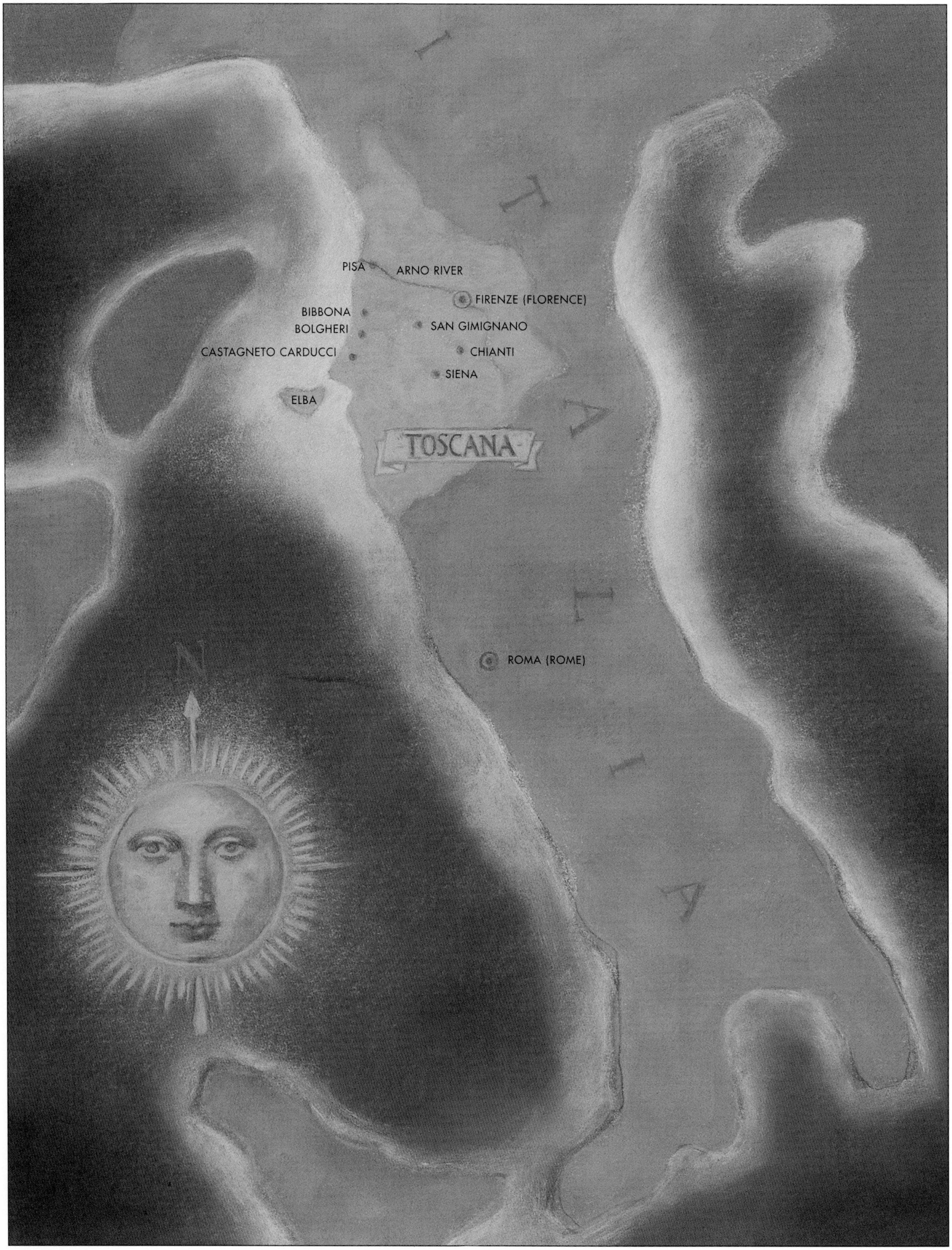

ITALIA
PISA
ARNO RIVER
FIRENZE (FLORENCE)
BIBBONA
BOLGHERI
SAN GIMIGNANO
CASTAGNETO CARDUCCI
CHIANTI
SIENA
ELBA
TOSCANA
N
ROMA (ROME)

T

Is for Toscana

Gary Kelley

Creative Editions

Mille grazie – Julie, Uwe, Steffi e Sebastian

Illustrations and text copyright © 2003 by Gary Kelley; Published in 2003 by Creative Editions, 123 South Broad Street, Mankato, MN 56001 USA. Creative Editions is an imprint of The Creative Company. Designed by Rita Marshall. All rights reserved. No part of the contents of this book may be reproduced by any means without the written permission of the publisher. Printed in Italy. **Library of Congress Cataloging-in-Publication Data**: Kelley, Gary. T Is for Toscana / by Gary Kelley, 1949–; Summary: An illustrated, alphabetical introduction to various objects, people, sites, and customs associated with Tuscany. ISBN 1-56846-177-1; 1. Tuscany (Italy)—Description and travel—Juvenile literature. 2. Alphabet books. [1. Tuscany (Italy)—Description and travel. 2. Alphabet books.] I. Title. DG734.23 K45 2003   [E]—dc21   2002031432

First Edition 5 4 3 2 1

Is for Toscana

About the Italian Alphabet

The Italian alphabet, like the English one, is based on Latin. English embraces the full twenty-six letters of the modern Latin alphabet, while Italian makes do with just twenty-one Latin letters (although J, K, W, X, and Y are hospitably allowed into the lexicon in the form of borrowed foreign words). Italians are as deft with language as they are with food and can combine these twenty-one letters in ways that produce a full menu of sound—placing U before another vowel to create the sound of a W, for example—making the five omitted letters unnecessary.

Although the Italian alphabet is the same throughout Italy, the words formed by these letters roll from the tongue differently depending on the region. The natives of Florence, in the heart of Tuscany, have always used a unique pronunciation that is probably rooted in the more flexible Greek-based alphabet of the Etruscans who settled the area in ancient times. Pronunciations throughout this book are given in this Tuscan style, which has spread to become one of the most common vernaculars in Italy.

Arno

Florence tolerates her river **Arno**. In winter it may flood, while in summer it runs nearly dry. Its most famous bridge, the Ponte Vecchio, has survived the tantrums of Mother Nature and human nature for more than six centuries.

Arno (AHR-noh)

B

Biciletta

In the narrow streets of hilltop towns such as Castagneto Carducci, recreation and transportation often turn on the wheels of a **Bicycle**.

Biciletta (Bee-chee-KLEH-tah)

C

Cipressi

A long, straight avenue of **Cypress** trees takes the traveler up from the coastal plain into the hills and to the medieval castle at Bolgheri.

Cipressi (Chee-PREH-see)

D

Duomo

The **Dome** of Santa Maria de Fiore in Florence is the most famous child of Filippo Brunelleschi (1377–1446), the father of Renaissance architecture.

Duomo (DWOH-moh)

E

Entrata

A weathered wooden door marks the **Entrance** to this centuries-old home, which is typical in the tiny village of Bibbona.

Entrata (En-TRAH-tah)

F

The communal **Fountain** is still a fixture in Tuscan neighborhoods. Today almost all are as dry as the summer countryside.

Fontana (Fohn-TAH-nah)

Fontana

G

Gelato

A sweet treat enjoyed in Siena's bustling town center, the Piazza del Campo, this is **Ice Cream** to write home about!

Gelato (Jeh-LAH-toh)

H

Hotel

The eighth letter of the Italian alphabet is seldom used. However, the English word **Hotel** has come to mean overnight lodging for the weary traveler throughout Tuscany.

Hotel (Oh-TEHL)

I

Isola

The **Island** of Elba, just off the Tuscan coast, is visited annually by thousands of tourists. Its most famous "tourist," Napoleon Bonaparte, visited from 1814 to 1815 as an exiled emperor.

Isola (EE-zoh-lah)

L

Leonardo

The world's best-known portrait, the *Mona Lisa*, was painted by Tuscan artist, architect, scientist, and inventor **Leonardo** da Vinci (1452–1519), the original "Renaissance Man."

Leonardo (Leh-oh-NAHR-doh)

M

Mercato

The lively, open-air **Market** is a circus for the senses—the smell of garlic, the color of ripe tomatoes, the sound of street musicians, the feel of fresh-baked bread, and the taste of sweet peaches.

Mercato (Mehr-KAH-toh)

N

Negozi

Afternoon streets are left to barking dogs and sightseers as most Tuscan **Shops** close for a few hours, allowing their keepers to enjoy a family meal and the siesta that follows.

Negozi (Neh-GOH-tsee)

Olivo

Tuscans are proud of their renowned **Olive** oil, made from the prized fruit that is harvested by hand, one tree at a time.

Olivo (Oh-LEE-voh)

P

Pisa

The tourist-friendly Leaning Tower of **Pisa** took one hundred seventy-six years to build… and has been leaning ever since construction began in the twelfth century.

Pisa (PEE-sah)

Wild boar roam the forests of Tuscany, rooting out their favorite delicacy, acorns dropped by spreading **Oak** trees.

Querci (KWEHR-chee)

Querci

R

Ruderi

Farmhouse **Ruins** haunt the hillsides and valleys, waiting to be restored by patient hands and reborn as stylish country villas.

Ruderi (ROO-deh-ree)

S

Spiaggia

Another day at the **Beach** draws to a close for this African basket merchant peddling his wares on the Etruscan Riviera.

Spiaggia (Spee-AHD-jah)

T

Torri

Soaring **Towers**, erected during the Middle Ages by rival noblemen with soaring egos, dominate the skyline of the postcard village of San Gimignano.

Torri (TOH-ree)

U

Uffizi

Thanks to the Medici family, the **Uffizi** Gallery in Florence is home to a vast collection of Italian Renaissance art, including the popular *Birth of Venus*, painted in 1485 by Sandro Botticelli.

Uffizi (OO-FEE-tsee)

V

Vigneti

The Chianti region is a patchwork of **Vineyards** that produce the grapes used to make world-class red wines.

Vigneti (Vee-NYEH-tee)

Z

Zuppa

The evening meal in Tuscany is often late, light, and simple: salt-free bread served with a meager **Soup**. Buon appetito!

Zuppa (TSOO-pah)

T

Tuscany

About Tuscany

Tuscany is a region of Italy that was settled around 1000 B.C. by an ancient tribe of people known as the Etruscans. It is a land of varied geography and splendid natural beauty. In the region's interior is a mountain range called the Apennines. The mountains give way to hilly lowlands that flank the river Arno, and the lowlands give way to a stark coastal plain called the Maremma. In the spring, Tuscany's rolling landscape is a lush green splashed with the red of poppies. In the summer, it is the rich gold of sunflowers and wheat. In the fall, it is the earthy brown of plowed fields.

This was the epicenter of the Renaissance. It was in Tuscany that da Vinci painted, Michelangelo sculpted, Dante wrote poetry, Machiavelli philosophized, and Galileo learned of gravity. This intellectual and artistic legacy is celebrated today in the renowned galleries of the cities of Florence, Pisa, and Siena. The countryside, too, tells the tale of Tuscany's past. It is dotted with centuries-old castles, fortresses, monasteries, and towers— some in ruin, others in use. Many of these medieval structures sit atop Roman ruins that sit atop Etruscan ruins.

Tuscan villages tend to be perched on hilltops. Away from the major cities, the rolling land is home to many such villages surrounded by stone farmhouses, sprawling vineyards, and groves of cypress trees and umbrella pines. Dirt roads wind their way between hills, passing dense forests that are home to wild boar, deer, and foxes, not to mention wild mushrooms that wait to be picked and tossed into cooking pots.

Tuscany's native population of three and a half million people grows slowly; no country in the world has a lower birthrate than Italy. Yet tourists and immigrants are more than willing to compensate for this. Most of Europe seems to vacation in August, a month in which Tuscany's population swells with *stranieri*, or foreigners. Visitors can explore by car or bicycle, though electric scooters are the vehicles of choice for locals. Most streets and alleys in Tuscan cities and villages are exceptionally narrow and difficult to navigate. Drivers are encouraged to park outside town walls and traverse the streets on foot or bicycle.

The attention bestowed on Tuscany's history and beauty is well-deserved, but this is also a land famous for food. The region's Mediterranean climate is perfect for growing wheat, olives, grapes, and vegetables. Many fields are also planted with corn and sunflowers or used to raise cattle, pigs, and poultry. Produced on mostly small farms, these foods are turned into the breads, pastas, sausages, olive oil, and wine for which Italian meals are so celebrated.

Tuscans enjoy life at a gentle and unhurried pace. The Italian word *domani* translates to English as "tomorrow," but in Tuscany means "sometime in the future." Tuscans tend to live by this unscheduled sense of time. In the biggest cities and smallest villages, afternoon streets are quiet as people catch some rest between lunch and supper. Leisure is important in Tuscany, as are friends. When companions part, they do not wave good-bye. They wave with palms up as if to say, "Come back."

Endnotes

Filippo Brunelleschi

In 1418, the grand Florence Cathedral was nearly complete after more than a century of construction. But one major obstacle remained: building a dome one hundred thirty-two feet in diameter over the cathedral. When cathedral officials announced a prize for the best dome design, a forty-one-year-old engineer and mathematical genius named Filippo Brunelleschi (1377–1446) stepped forward to solve the problem and claim the prize. He abandoned traditional framing and buttressing techniques and instead devised a method of placing bricks in a herringbone pattern between stone beams. The result, completed sixteen years later, was a marvelous freestanding dome. The doming of the Florence Cathedral earned Brunelleschi lasting fame, but his legacy as an architectural pioneer was also forged by his groundbreaking designs for churches, palaces, and fortresses.

Leonardo da Vinci

Leonardo da Vinci (1452–1519) was born near the small Tuscan town of Vinci, the son of a lawyer and a peasant woman. During his sixty-seven years of life, he established himself as the most versatile genius of the Renaissance period. Da Vinci painted such masterpieces as the *Mona Lisa* and *The Last Supper*, but he regarded his skills as a painter and sculptor secondary to those as an architect, scientist, and inventor. All people of prominence wanted to bask in his brilliance; during his lifetime he spent time as the court artist of Milan duke Ludovico Sforza, guest of Pope Leo X at the Vatican palace, and "first painter and engineer and architect" of French king Francis I. When he died, he left behind thousands of notebook pages filled with sketches and notes on flying machines and other ideas centuries ahead of their time.

The Medici family

Medici is the name of a prominent family who ruled the city of Florence—and, for a time, Tuscany—from the early 1400s until 1734. In the early 1300s, the family moved from the countryside to Florence and became bankers and merchants. A century later, after founding a bank in Rome, their fortunes skyrocketed. Though private citizens who held no official office (until 1532, when the family became the dukes of Florence), the Medici controlled all affairs in Florence. Their kindness toward the common people made them popular, and their wealth earned them friends in high places. Four members of the family became popes, and at the peak of their power, the Medici were as rich as any kings or princes of Europe. The most famous members of the family were Cosimo the Elder (1389–1464), whose shrewd business sense built up the family empire, and his grandson Lorenzo "the Magnificent" (1449–1492), whose love of the arts helped Renaissance painters and sculptors to flourish.

Sandro Botticelli

Artist Sandro Botticelli (1445–1510) was born Alessandro di Mariano Filipepi but for unknown reasons adopted the nickname of his older brother Giovanni, "Il Botticello" ("The Little Barrel"), early in life. His paintings are known for their clear lines, delicate color, and poetic feeling and are generally more melancholy than the paintings of other Renaissance artists. Early in his career, he focused largely on mythological subjects, creating such classic paintings as the *Birth of Venus*. As his fame spread, he was hired to paint portraits of members of the powerful Medici family and received commissions to create works for all of the major churches in Florence. Later in life, he painted only religious works and was among the elite artists asked to paint wall frescoes in the Vatican's Sistine Chapel in Rome.